Young Queen Elizabeth

Young Queen Elizabeth

by Francene Sabin
illustrated by John Lawn

Troll Associates

Library of Congress Cataloging-in-Publication Data

Sabin, Francene.
   Young Queen Elizabeth / by Francene Sabin; illustrated by John
Lawn.
     p.   cm.
   Summary: Focuses on the childhood of the queen who, during her
forty-five-year reign, changed England from a minor country into a
world power.
   ISBN 0-8167-1785-0 (lib. bdg.)   ISBN 0-8167-1786-9 (pbk.)
   1. Elizabeth I, Queen of England, 1533-1603—Childhood and youth—
Juvenile literature.   2. Great Britain—History—Henry VIII,
1509-1547—Juvenile literature.   3. Great Britain—Kings and rulers—
Biography—Juvenile literature. [1. Elizabeth I, Queen of
England, 1533-1603—Childhood and youth. 2. Kings, queens, rulers,
etc.] I. Lawn, John, ill. II. Title.
DA355.S23 1990
942.05 ′5 ′092—dc20
[B]
[92]   89-33941

Young
Queen Elizabeth

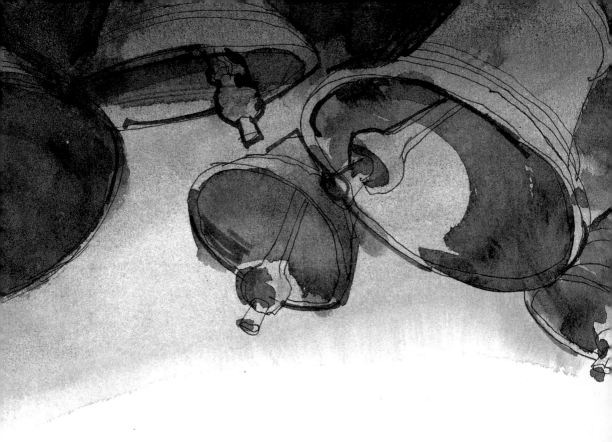

The night sky glowed golden red over London. Light blazed from hundreds of bonfires throughout the city. Church bells rang out. There was dancing and feasting in almost every street in the English capital. And the joyous cry of "Long live Princess Elizabeth!" echoed through the night. The celebration, on September 7, 1533, honored the birth of Princess Elizabeth, daughter of King Henry the Eighth and Queen Anne Boleyn.

7

There were special reasons for the grand celebration. First of all, Elizabeth was a strong and healthy baby. That was certainly a reason for great joy. In those days, there was very little medical knowledge. Many babies died at birth, and only the strongest survived.

There was another cause for joy. Elizabeth was a truly English princess. King Henry already had a daughter, seventeen-year-old Mary. But Catherine, Mary's mother and King Henry's first wife, was Spanish. That meant Mary was half-English and half-Spanish.

England and Spain were great rivals. The English people were afraid of being ruled by a half-Spanish queen. If Mary became queen, would she be loyal to England or Spain? Would she make England a colony of Spain? Would she destroy centuries of English history? Those questions hung over England like a cloud.

But now there was an all-English princess. There could never be a doubt of her loyalty to her country and people!

King Henry had also longed for a truly English heir. But he did not join in the celebration on the night of Elizabeth's birth. In fact, he was furious. His anger was felt throughout Windsor Castle. Henry had wanted a son, and his astrologers had promised him one. Astrologers studied the positions of the stars and believed such positions influenced events on earth. The astrologers' predictions, though not scientific, were taken seriously by many people at the time. And Henry was no exception.

The king raged at everyone in sight. He blamed his astrologers. He also blamed his royal advisers. He said they should have stopped him from divorcing Catherine and marrying Anne. Most of all, he blamed Anne for failing to give him the son he wanted.

Nobody could tell how King Henry would act from one minute to the next. First, he was furious about Elizabeth's birth. Then he arranged a magnificent christening ceremony and enjoyed every moment of it. A day later, he exploded with fury at having to pay for the feast after the christening.

These swift changes of the king's mood made life difficult for everyone around him, especially his family. So it was lucky for Elizabeth that she did not see her father very often.

The custom was to raise royal children apart from their parents. The royal nursery wasn't even in the same castle as the king and queen's. Right from birth, Elizabeth had her own large staff of servants.

There was a lady governess, who was in charge. There were yeomen, the young noblemen who acted as servants to the young princess. There were grooms to care for the horses in Elizabeth's stables. There were officers of the pantry, who bought and prepared food for Elizabeth and her household. There were even three people whose job it was to rock the royal cradle.

There were also two nurses. The choice of nurses was very important. In those days it was believed that a baby would pick up all the faults, as well as the good traits, of the nurse. There was no work for a cross-eyed nurse or one with an odd voice. People believed the baby would "catch" cross-eye, an odd voice, or any other problem the nurse suffered.

A royal nurse was watched every minute. Everything she ate or drank was carefully planned. People thought that what you ate shaped your temper and behavior. So the nurse had to eat things that would supposedly make her sweet and proper. The baby in her care would then grow up with these admired qualities.

To protect the royal baby's health, there were very strict rules. The royal servants were not allowed to go into the city of London. And Londoners who came to deliver food, tools, fabrics, and other merchandise were not allowed inside the walls of the castle. They did all their trading through an iron grille in the castle gate.

The great fear of the time was the plague. Plague is a disease caused by bacteria. The bacteria are carried by fleas. Plague-carrying fleas pass on the disease when they bite humans or animals. Plague is rare in our modern world. We prevent it through cleanliness, and we can cure it with antibiotics.

But in Elizabeth's time, plague was a terrifying and mysterious force. When it struck, it wiped out thousands of people at a time. So the royal household tried to guard against this disease.

Nothing they did, however, would have stopped the plague. That is because people did not know that it was carried by fleas. So they paid no attention to cleanliness.

Sixteenth-century people had no idea that it was important to bathe and to keep their homes clean. Even the royal nursery was filthy. There were fleas everywhere. They lived on the dogs and cats that wandered freely through the rooms. Fleas were also on the humans who cared for the infant princess.

Princess Elizabeth, like babies throughout England, had red flea bites on her face and body. But this was so common that nobody paid any attention to it. And fleas weren't the only health problem. Stone castles were very cold, damp, and drafty. A fireplace might warm one small part of a large room, but not most of it. Adults wore heavy clothing, even with fur, indoors and out. Nevertheless, coughs and colds were common.

The royal castle also had a terrible smell. There were no bathrooms and no running water. Garbage was left to rot outside the royal kitchen. Children and grown-ups walked around with flowers or perfumed handkerchiefs. They sniffed at these sweet-smelling objects often.

When the smells and filth became unbearable, the royal household packed up and moved. Sometimes, they would move to another royal castle. Other times, they would pay a long visit to the home of a duke or earl. Of course, it was a great honor to have a royal visitor. But a royal visitor brought servants and soldiers, horses, dogs, clowns, doctors, musicians—a huge crowd. And the nobleman had to feed and house everyone. It was a very expensive honor!

When the royal family left one of their castles, every room was cleaned. In fact, this was the only time a castle was aired and scrubbed.

Even though she was surrounded by dirt and disease, Elizabeth grew into a healthy, pretty child. She had beautiful coloring—rosy cheeks, a clear and creamy skin, and bright red hair. The pretty princess was a delight to the English people.

Elizabeth was also fortunate to have a good governess. She was Lady Margaret Bryan. Lady Bryan was as kind to Elizabeth as if she were the child's own mother. That was a good thing, because Elizabeth had so little to do with her parents. As a matter of fact, when she talked about it years later, she could remember being with both parents only two times.

19

The first was a happy occasion, when Elizabeth was two and a half years old. Queen Anne was going to have a baby. King Henry told everyone this child would be a boy. He was so sure of this that he even gave a huge party. For the party, the king wore shiny yellow clothes. He had Princess Elizabeth dressed in a matching yellow gown.

Elizabeth never forgot that party. Her tall, powerful father carried her around, showing her off to everyone. He kissed her often and called her the prettiest lass in the world.

The second occasion Elizabeth remembered was
a very unhappy one. The son Henry wanted was
born dead. The king was in a rage. He turned this
fury against the queen. He had her put on trial
for treason. The royal councilors found her guilty,
and the king ordered her to be beheaded.

Several days before the execution, Queen Anne made a last plea for her life. A nobleman who was present later wrote these words to Elizabeth: "Alas, I shall never forget the sorrow I felt when I saw the sainted queen, your mother. She was carrying you in her arms. She came to the most serene king, your father, in Greenwich Palace. She brought you to him in the courtyard as he stood at the open window. She begged for her life to be spared for your sake."

The king would not change his mind. Anne was taken to the Tower of London, where she was put to death. Just one day later, King Henry married again. The new queen was Jane Seymour. Henry hoped that Queen Jane would give birth to a healthy son to inherit the throne.

Elizabeth became a forgotten princess. The king did not want to see her or hear her name. In time, she outgrew the clothes her mother, Queen Anne, had bought for her. No new ones were made. Finally, Lady Bryan sent a letter to the king. In it, she begged for dresses, shoes, petticoats, nightgowns, and other articles of clothing for the princess.

King Henry's secretary sent a small amount of money. With it, he included a letter telling Lady Bryan not to ask for money again. Elizabeth, he wrote, was to live without luxuries. Her mother had angered the king, and for this reason the child must suffer too.

Elizabeth's life changed again when she was four years old. Queen Jane gave birth to a boy, who was named Edward. The king was very pleased. He even allowed Elizabeth to be treated better. She was dressed in fine clothes again. She was given a larger staff of servants, thirty-two in all. And a new governess, Katherine Champernowne, replaced Lady Bryan. Again, Elizabeth was lucky—her new governess was a well-educated woman and an excellent teacher.

Princess Elizabeth was a very bright child. By the time she was six, she could read and write as well as most adults of that time. She also knew Latin. In addition to Katherine Champernowne, the young princess had several teachers. One taught her mathematics. Another taught her Italian and French. Still others taught her music, art, and dancing.

There were no textbooks. Instead, the Bible was used for teaching. Elizabeth first learned to read the Bible. She learned to write by copying lines from the Bible. She read the Bible in Latin. Then she learned to translate Biblical passages from Latin into English and from English into French.

The young princess did read other books, but not many. There were no children's books then. The books Elizabeth read were always very serious.

Sixteenth-century children were brought up strictly. They even had to look serious. A philosopher of that time wrote that laughter meant empty-headedness or wickedness. A proper child, he said, might smile a bit, but not much nor for very long. Also, when a child laughed, the mouth should be covered by a handkerchief. And most people agreed with him.

Laughter wasn't the only thing to be avoided
by children. They were also told not to wrinkle
the nose, twist the mouth, frown, yawn, sniffle,
or sneeze. They must not jump around, play, or
act like children at all. Children were considered
to be small adults, and they were expected to act
like adults.

When children acted like children, they were
called wicked. Punishment for being wicked could
be very severe. Youngsters obeyed the rules
because they were afraid of being punished.

Princess Elizabeth had more reason than most children to fear punishment. King Henry did nothing to control his anger. When he was angry enough, he sent people to prison or to be executed. He did not even spare his own family. Of King Henry's six wives, for example, two he divorced and banished from England and two he had executed. Another died during childbirth. Only his sixth and last wife, Catherine Parr, outlived him—by a year.

King Henry's violence made a deep impression on Princess Elizabeth. She grew up afraid to trust anyone. And she never let anyone become close to her. Many times when Elizabeth was queen, it looked as if she might marry. But each time she changed her mind. And each time she offered a reason for turning down the proposal of marriage.

If she married a foreign king, Elizabeth said, it
might be bad for England. A foreigner could make
England a colony of his own country. Many
English people agreed with Elizabeth, and they
accepted this explanation.

The English people wanted Elizabeth to marry
an Englishman. They wanted her to have children. If Elizabeth didn't have children, who would
rule England when she died? Would the French,
Spanish, or Scottish take over England? Would
there be wars fought over the English throne?

Elizabeth understood the fears of her people.
But her own fear was greater. Any husband,
English or foreign, might try to take the throne
from her. He might even condemn her to death,
as her father had done to her mother. This fear
ruled the queen of England as strongly as she
ruled her country.

Elizabeth's feelings were not surprising. Until
she became queen, she never really felt safe.
Before King Henry died in 1547, there was always
the danger of his anger. After Henry's death, nine-
year-old Prince Edward became king. He was a
nice boy and liked his thirteen-year-old half-sister,
Elizabeth. But because he was still a child, he had
no real power. England was actually ruled by
Edward's uncles and cousins. They were not
related to Elizabeth and did not feel any loyalty
to her. Elizabeth wasn't mistreated by them, but
she still lived in fear. Wisely, the teen-age princess
tried not to be noticed too much.

Elizabeth stayed in the country, far from London. There, her days were filled with studying. Her education was excellent. The finest professors from Cambridge University were happy to teach the princess. That was not just because she was the princess. Elizabeth was a brilliant student. She spoke and read French, Italian, Latin, Greek, and Spanish, as well as her native English. She knew a great deal of mathematics and science. She wrote music, played more than one musical instrument, and sang in a clear, sweet voice.

Elizabeth did not think she would ever be queen. Still, she studied the art of government with special care. She loved her country and had dreams of glory for England. She studied geography and imagined English colonies in the New World. She studied military history and dreamed of a mighty English navy that would rule the seas. In the quiet of her country home, Elizabeth dedicated herself to learning and thinking. And these years of intense study would one day be put to good use.

In 1553, fifteen-year-old King Edward the Sixth died. Who would take the throne of England? Just before the young king's death, he was convinced to name a cousin, Lady Jane Grey, as his successor. She declared herself queen the day he died.

Princess Elizabeth did nothing, but her older half-sister, Mary, acted. She refused to accept Lady Jane Grey as the new queen. Instead, Mary gathered an army and overthrew Lady Jane's government. In August 1553, Mary Tudor became queen of England.

Many of the English people did not want Mary on the throne. She was half-Spanish, and this bothered them. It bothered them even more when Mary married Prince Philip of Spain. The threat of Spanish conquest was growing every day. More and more, the English wanted Elizabeth as their queen. Very soon, Mary learned of this. She blamed Elizabeth for what the people said. She accused Elizabeth of plotting to overthrow the government.

Elizabeth was not involved in any plot. And she told Mary, in letters and in person, that she wasn't plotting anything. But Mary was furious at Elizabeth's popularity. Mary had waited many years to become queen, and she would not let her pretty half-sister take the crown from her now.

In March 1554, two councilors came to escort
Elizabeth to prison in the Tower of London.
Elizabeth was shocked. She could not believe
that Mary was responsible for this. Elizabeth
asked to be brought to the queen, but Mary
would not see her. Elizabeth then wrote a letter
to Mary, saying that she was innocent and faith-
ful to the throne.

The letter covered a page and a half. And where nothing was written, Elizabeth drew slanting lines. This, she explained, was to make sure that nobody could write bad things and say that they were her words. It was clever of Elizabeth to do this, but not surprising. She had been well trained not to trust messengers, councilors, or even relatives.

The letter did no good. The twenty-year-old Elizabeth was taken to the Tower. To make it worse, she was brought in through the Traitor's Gate. Only condemned prisoners were taken to the Tower that way. It was a terrible disgrace for Elizabeth.

She remained in the Tower prison for two months. Every day she feared her execution would take place. But Mary did not dare to have her sister killed. The people were getting angrier. They might rise up in rebellion if the well-loved Elizabeth was put to death. So Mary freed Elizabeth and sent her off to the country.

In November 1558, Mary died, and Elizabeth's life of fear finally ended. Elizabeth became queen of England. Now all her years of preparation proved of value.

For the full length of her long reign, lasting until her death in 1603, England flourished. It became the most powerful nation on earth. Under Elizabeth, a powerful English navy ruled the oceans. It destroyed the Spanish fleet in 1588, and with it Spain's place as a major force among nations.

Elizabeth also encouraged her navy to range far and wide, to explore the known and unknown world. These explorations led to the development of colonies in North America. In a sense, American history began during the reign of Queen Elizabeth the First.

Queen Elizabeth's years on the throne are important for other reasons. England enjoyed many years of prosperity and peace during her reign. Elizabeth encouraged the arts as no ruler had before her. It was an age when the writing of plays and poetry blossomed. William Shakespeare, one of the greatest writers of all time, produced his masterpieces during the Elizabethan Age. In fact, a number of his plays were specifically written for the queen to see.

Queen Elizabeth the First died on March 24, 1603. In the forty-five years she ruled England, she accomplished great things. The England she began to rule in 1558 was just a small island, always in danger from other countries. The England she built was a far-reaching power.

Queen Elizabeth the First planted the seeds that would grow into the British Empire—an island nation that at one time ruled almost half the world!

Date Due			

cop 1